Five Little Ducks

WRITTEN BY
VIVIAN FRENCH

ILLUSTRATED BY
PAUL DOWLING

WALKER BOOKS
AND SUBSIDIARIES

LONDON • BOSTON • SYDNEY

First published 2001 by Walker Books Ltd
87 Vauxhall Walk, London SE11 5HJ

2 4 6 8 10 9 7 5 3 1

Text © 2001 Vivian French
Illustrations © 2001 Paul Dowling

This book has been typeset in Century Old Style

Printed in Hong Kong

British Library Cataloguing in Publication Data:
a catalogue record for this book is
available from the British Library

ISBN 0-7445-8310-1

Notes for Children

This book is a little different from other picture books.
You will be sharing it with other people and telling
the story together.

You can read

this line

this line

or this line.

Even when someone else is reading, try to follow
the words. It will help when it's your turn!

Five little ducks

Went swimming one day

Splish splash splish!

Splish splash splish!

Over the hills
And far away.

Mummy Duck said

"Quack! Quack! Quack! Quack!"

But one little duck

Went off to hide

And four little ducks

Came swimming back.

Four little ducks

Went walking one day

Pit pat pit pat!

Pit pat pit pat!

Over the bridge

And far away.

Mummy Duck said

"Quack! Quack! Quack! Quack!"

But one little duck

Went off to hide

And three little ducks

Came walking back.

Three little ducks

Went skipping one day

Skip hop skip!

Skip hop skip!

Down by the reeds

And far away.

Mummy Duck said

"Quack! Quack! Quack! Quack!"

But one little duck

Went off to hide

And two little ducks

Came skipping back.

Two little ducks

Went jumping one day

Up up over!

Up up over!

Over the rocks

And far away.

Mummy Duck said

"Quack! Quack! Quack! Quack!"

But one little duck

Went off to hide

And one little duck

Came jumping back.

One little duck

Went paddling one day

Splash splosh splash!

Splosh splash splosh!

Into the pond

And far away.

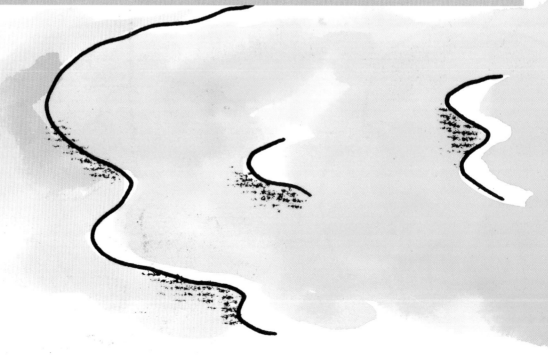

Mummy Duck said

"Quack! Quack! Quack! Quack!"

But NO little ducks

Came paddling back.

"QUACK!" said Mummy Duck
"PLEASE come back!"

And one little

Two little

Three little

Four little

Five little ducks

Came splashing back!

One Mummy Duck

Went swimming one day

Over the hills and far away.

Mummy Duck sang

"Quack! Quack! Quack! Quack!"

To the five little ducks

Asleep on her back.

Notes for Teachers

Story Plays are written and presented in a way that encourages children to read aloud together. They are exciting stories, told in strongly patterned language which gives children the chance to practise at a vital stage of their reading development. Sharing stories in this way makes reading an active and enjoyable process, and one that draws in even the reticent reader.

The story is told by three different voices, divided into three colours so that each child can easily read his or her part. When there are more than three children in a group, there is an ideal opportunity for paired reading. Partnering a more experienced reader with a less experienced one can be very supportive and provides a learning experience for both children.

Story Plays encourage children to share in the reading of a whole text in a collaborative and interactive way. This makes them perfect for group and guided reading activities. Children will find they need to pay close attention to the print and punctuation, and to use the meaning of the whole story in order to read it with expression and a real sense of voice.